Calligraphic Designs

Mimi Armstrong

Stemmer House
PUBLISHERS, INC.
OWINGS MILLS, MARYLAND

Introduction

THIS BOOK IS AN ATTEMPT TO MERGE calligraphy with another graphic form, drawing.

The combination is, of course, nothing new. For over a thousand years when books were made by hand, page after page of calligraphy was decorated with small drawings. These were painted with bright colors, and many were illuminated with gold leaf. The drawings and the writing were usually wrapped around each other partially, rather than being two separate parts put on one page. The scribe did the writing first, leaving gaps for the illuminator to fill. Although only a few pages in this book are medieval in style, my goal has been to blend and unify pictures with writing in the old manner.

Calligrams, or pictures made of or with writing, seem to fall into three general types. The first kind is made by selecting a letter in a word and exaggerating or elongating that letter to make a picture of the subject. For instance, the tail of the "g" in the phrase "grape vine" could be extended and decorated with grape leaves growing from it. One oftens finds this sort of calligram used for logos.

In the second type, the writing itself makes a border or outline of a shape. A Valentine's poem might be written in the outline of a heart. Simple shapes without too many points seem to work best. It is always horrifying when the proud calligrapher's shape is a mystery to the viewers! Skill and lively writing will protect this kind of calligram from being too trite.

The third kind masses the writing to make the whole filled-in shape. For this kind of calligram, legibility is sometimes sacrificed to the overall shape. Heavy, dense writing makes a stronger form than light, airy lettering. Forcing the letters to fit the given shape will sometimes cause distortion of individual letters. A contrast of weights and styles within one shape can create interesting textures.

In finding quotations that would suit this book that I was writing but not WRITING, I luckily hit upon anthologies of children's poetry. Here were quotations about THINGS, real things like soup and cows and oranges. I mulled over poems for weeks, sometimes longer, before the final selection. By the time I chose the passages, I felt so comfortable with them that ideas for accompanying drawings happily slipped right out on paper. The execution of the ideas was not quite so easy!

Every art student hears a thousand times that one must work constantly over the entire piece stage by stage and not fuss with one tiny corner at a time. Otherwise, the finished work may have bits of exquisite painting or drawing, but end up jarring and disjointed.

For these drawings, therefore, I used a method of designing that for me and my illumination students has been surefire. With a regular #2 pencil I rapidly sketched several ideas at the correct size. The most promising one I kept, and did another sketch with a quick back-and-forth movement, so that the strokes were sloppy and overlapping. But, at least, the idea was out of the head and on the paper.

Then I took a sheet of tracing paper and a harder pencil, either a 3H or 4H and very sharp, and went over that best drawing, making a single line rather than an overlapping thick line. This good line might be right over the sketchy one or else outside of it, but it would definitely be a correction of the rough beginning. Rarely, though, would this single tracing give a good result. Usually it took four or five or even six tracings to get a good drawing. Each one I put over the previous one, unless that one was not good. Then I might go back over an earlier version.

Finally, after much mulling and weighing and squinting, and constantly reminding myself to think of how the writing would fit, I knew when the drawing was fine. When the flow of curves was pleasing and graceful, with the white space and black space just right, the drawing was ready for transfer.

I rubbed Armenian bole, a red-brown powdered clay, on the back of my tracing. After gently taping the clay-backed drawing to my good paper, I went over it with my hard pencil. Corrections were still possible. When I lifted the tracing paper off, there was a nice red brown outline of my drawing on paper, ready for pen and ink. I then went over my drawing with India ink, using a crow quill pen, and touched up flaws with white paint.

Choosing the styles and sizes of writing for a page is hard. I would rather do my own work, no matter how poor, than a lukewarm version of someone else's. Therefore, though I have collections of famous calligraphers' alphabet sheets that I keep for teaching examples, I hate using them.

So I did not plug in an alphabet from an exemplar sheet. My goal was to design a particular version of a particular kind of alphabet that was for that page alone. I experimented with pen angle, letter height, letter shape, pressure and rhythm.

Most finished calligraphy emerges in this way from a thousand tiny decisions, which all seem fairly crucial at the time. No matter how fast and furiously one works, each pen stroke is a crucial decision. As with the drawings, there is always the constant evaluation. A good calligrapher is not only diligent, but also must have a tolerance for the tedium of revisions!

Truthfully, I am not a perfectionist at all. My calligraphy has always been brimming with inconsistencies and less than perfect letter shapes and it does not bother me a bit.

I loved making this book. Calligraphy at its best purifies, clarifies the words. Hastily handwritten on a paper scrap or typed, the same words might be passed over, given no thought whatsoever, even if they are sterling. But written out vigorously with life and character, the same words will make the reader pause and reflect. Then calligraphy has truly done its job. And if calligraphy can make people smile, so much the better.

The Baltimore-Washington area in which I've learned and practiced calligraphy is justly renowned for its calligraphic traditions. The Walters Art Gallery in Baltimore has a grand collection of illuminated manuscripts, with outstanding exhibitions. The Washington Calligraphers Guild has a strong program with its lectures, workshops, the acclaimed magazine "Scripsit," and its good fellowship. The high standards and solid teaching set by transplanted British calligrapher Sheila Waters have been a great boon to calligraphers here. I feel very fortunate to have had this abundance of calligraphic riches surrounding me.

I would like to thank the following people: Chere Jarrell and Rose Folsom, Ieuan Rees and the Tuesday Group, Anne and Bob Lane of Calligraphics, Ink, Wendy Glaubitz and Karen Strassburg and Jane, Stephen and Dean Armstrong. I would also like to thank Barbara Holdridge of Stemmer House Publishers for asking me to do this book and for giving me the freedom to do it as I wished.

Annapolis
August 1983

M.A.

List of Quotations and Authors

Thank you, God, for a hundred things
    Anonymous
Matthew, Mark, Luke and John   Anonymous
Oh, peacock brilliant, peacock bright
    Mimi Armstrong
Daisies pied, violets blue   William Shakespeare
Gather ye rosebuds while ye may   Robert Herrick
How doth the little busy bee   Isaac Watts
How doth the little crocodile   Anonymous
King David and King Solomon   James Ball Naylor
I've known rivers   Langston Hughes
Why don't you speak for yourself, John?
    Henry Wadsworth Longfellow
Early to bed and early to rise
    Benjamin Franklin
Roses of sunshine, violets of dew   Anonymous
The cock is crowing   William Wordsworth
The moon on the one hand   Hilaire Belloc
But Noah found grace   Genesis, The Bible
All along the backwater   Kenneth Grahame
We, who play under the pines
    Elizabeth Coatsworth
The kitchen's the cosiest place   Anonymous

Beautiful soup, so rich and green   Lewis Carroll
What a wonderful bird the frog are   Anonymous
Dingty, diddlety, my mammy's maid   Anonymous
The Queen of Hearts   Anonymous
The King of Hearts   Anonymous
The Robin is the one   Emily Dickinson
Glory be to God on high   Nahum Tate
    (This is from the Carol: While shepherds
    watched their flocks.)
One lime in Alfriston   Anonymous
Before the falling summer sun
    William Wordsworth
Wrens and robins   Christina Rossetti
Oh! How I love, on a fair summer's eve
    John Keats
Do you carrot all for me?   Anonymous
You are a peach   Anonymous
The world is empty   Goethe
When the wind is in the east   Anonymous
Small April sobbed   Anonymous
The friendly cow all red and white
    R. L. Stevenson
The world is so full   R. L. Stevenson

FOR M.M.B. AND S.H.B.

FOR THE SUN THAT SHINES AND THE RAIN THAT DROPS · FOR ICE CREAM AND RAISINS AND LOLLIPOPS AMEN Thank you, God for a hundred things · for the flower that blooms · for the bird that sings · for the lollipops AMEN

BLESSED GUARDIAN ANGELS KEEP ME SAFE FROM DANGER WHILE ANGELS ROUND MY HEAD · ONE TO WATCH, ONE TO PRAY AND TWO TO BEAR MY SOUL AWAY · BLESSED

MATTHEW, MARK, LUKE AND JOHN GUARD THE BED THAT I LIE ON · FOUR CORNERS TO MY BED · FOUR I SLEEP · AMEN · THE LULLABY OF THE FOUR EVANGELISTS:

Oh, peacock brilliant · Peacock bright · Tail of green and golden light ·

DAISIES PIED, VIOLETS BLUE, LADYSMOCKS ALL SILVER WHITE &

GATHER YE ROSEBUDS WHILE YE MAY, OLD TIME IS STILL A-FLYING; AND THIS SAME FLOWER THAT SMILES TODAY SOON WILL BE DYING

CUCKOO BIRDS OF YELLOW HUE PAINT THE GARDEN WITH DELIGHT

How doth the little busy bee
improve each shining hour,
and gather honey all the day
from every opening flower.

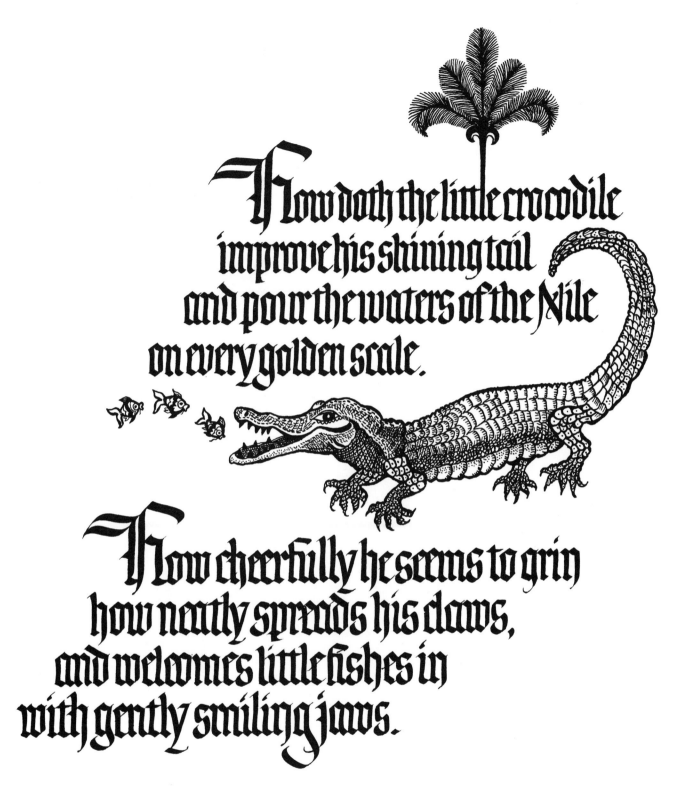

How doth the little crocodile
improve his shining tail
and pour the waters of the Nile
on every golden scale.

How cheerfully he seems to grin
how neatly spreads his claws,
and welcomes little fishes in
with gently smiling jaws.

King David and King Solomon led merry, merry lives, with many, many lady friends and many, many wives; But when old age crept over them—with many, many qualms, King Solomon wrote the Proverbs and King David wrote the Psalms.

LANGSTON HUGHES

I've known rivers: I've known rivers ancient as the world and older than the flow of human blood in human veins. My soul has grown deep like the rivers. I bathed in the Euphrates when dawns were young. I built my hut near the Congo and it lulled me to sleep. I looked upon the Nile and raised the pyramids above it. I've known rivers: Ancient, dusky rivers. My soul has grown deep like the rivers.

PHILA · DELPHIA

Early to bed and early to rise, makes a man healthy, wealthy & wise God helps them that help themselves Work as if you were to live a hundred years, pray as if you were to die tomorrow Little strokes fell great oaks He that riseth late must trot all day The cat in gloves catches no mice Some are weatherwise, some are otherwise An empty bag cannot stand upright The used key is always bright.

POOR RICHARD'S ALMANAC

THE COCK IS CROWING·THE STREAM IS
FLOWING·THE
SMALL BIRDS TWITTER·THE LAKE DOTH
GLITTER·THERE'S JOY IN
THE MOUNTAINS·THERE'S LIFE IN THE
FOUNTAINS·SMALL CLOUDS ARE
SAILING·BLUE SKY PREVAILING
THE RAIN IS
OVER AND GONE

William Wordsworth

Roses
of sunshine·Violets
of dew·Angels in
heaven know
I love
you

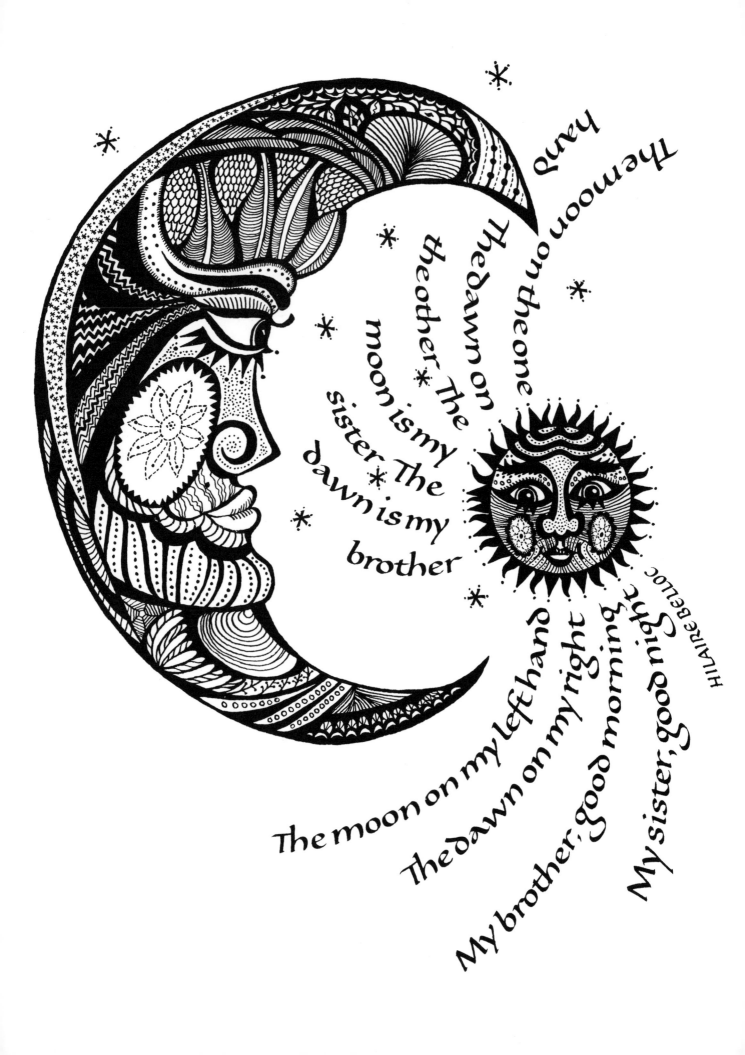

The moon on the one hand
The dawn on the other
The moon is my sister
The dawn is my brother

The moon on my left hand
The dawn on my right
My brother, good morning
My sister, good night

HILAIRE BELLOC

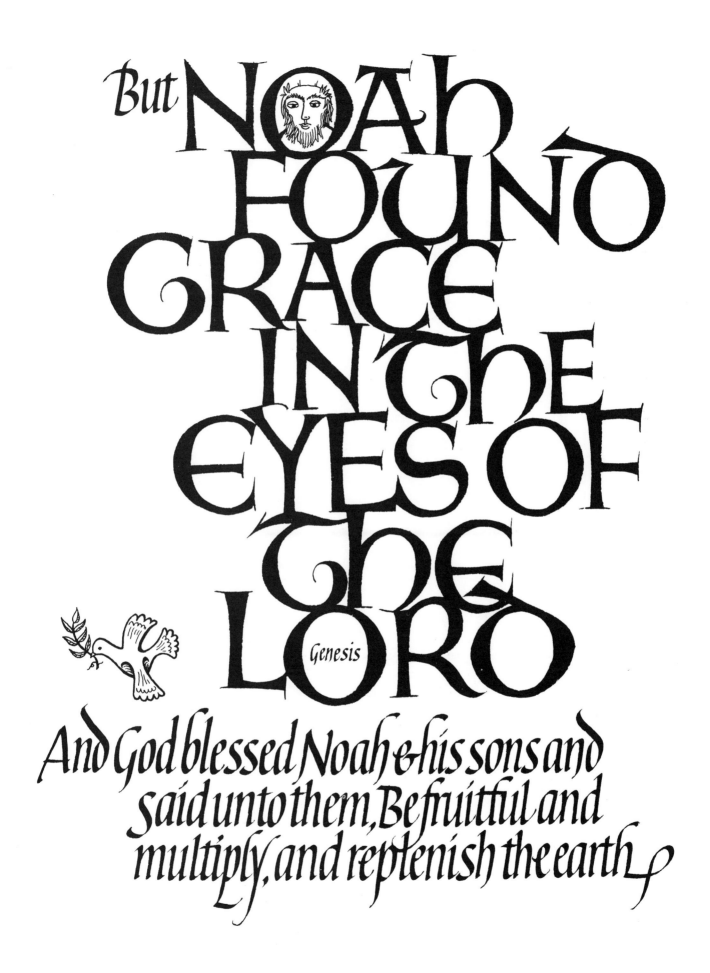

But NOAH FOUND GRACE IN THE EYES OF THE LORD

Genesis

And God blessed Noah & his sons and said unto them, Be fruitful and multiply, and replenish the earth.

All along the backwater
Through the rushes tall,
Ducks are a-dabbling,
Up tails all!

High in the blue above
Swifts whirl and call—
We are down a-dabbling
Up tails all
KENNETH GRAHAME

Ducks' tails, drakes' tails,
Yellow feet a-quiver,
Yellow bills all out of sight
Busy in the river.

Everyone for what he likes·
We like to be
Heads down, tails up,
Dabbling free!

Slushy green undergrowth
Where the roach swim—
Here we keep our larder
Cool and full and dim!

WE, WHO PLAY UNDER the pines, we who dance in the snow that shines blue in the light of the moon, sometimes halt as we go— stand with our ears erect to gaze at the golden world

ELIZABETH COATSWORTH

The kitchen's the cosiest place that I know

THE KETTLE IS SINGING

THE STOVE IS AGLOW

Beautiful Soup, so rich and green
Waiting in a hot tureen
Who for such dainties would
not stoop? Soup of the evening
BEAUTIFUL SOUP

LEWIS

CARROLL

What a wonderful bird the frog are.
When he stand, he sit almost.
When he hop, he fly almost.
He ain't got no sense hardly.
He ain't got no tail hardly either.
When he sit, he sit on what
he ain't got almost.

The Queen of Hearts
She made some tarts

All on a summer's day •
The Knave of Hearts
He stole the tarts • And took them clean away

The King of Hearts called for the tarts • And beat the Knave full sore • The Knave of Hearts Brought back the tarts And vowed he'd steal no more

Glory be to God on high, and to the earth be peace Goodwill henceforth from heaven to men begin and never cease

One lime in Alfriston made sweet,
SO SWEET, THE AUGUST NIGHT,
That all the air along the street,
THE SHADOWED AIR IN THE SHADOWED STREET,
Was swimming in delight.

If any bee had lingered there,
SHE MIGHT HAVE SPENT HER TIME,
In filling combs from that fragrant air,
HER GOLDEN COMBS FROM THE GOLDEN AIR,
And never seen the lime.

WRENS & ROBINS

WRENS AND ROBINS IN THE HEDGE
WRENS AND ROBINS HERE AND THERE
BUILDING · PERCHING · FLUTTERING
CHRISTINA EVERYWHERE ROSSETTI

Oh! How I love, on a fair summer's eve,
When streams of light pour down
the golden west,
And on the balmy zephyrs tranquil rest
The silver clouds, far-far away to leave
All meaner thoughts, and take
A sweet reprieve from little cares.

JOHN KEATS

THE WORLD'S EMPTY
if one thinks only of mountains, rivers & cities
BUT TO KNOW SOMEONE
here and there who feels and thinks with us,
AND WHO, THO DISTANT,
is close to us in spirit —
THIS MAKES THE
EARTH AN inhabited
GARDEN

Goethe

SMALL APRIL, PLEASE GIVE ME A RAINBOW, I SOBBED: "I'M GOING TO CRY." APRIL GAVE ME A CLOUD TO WIPE MY EYE. THEN, APRIL FOOL: SHE LAUGHED INSTEAD AND SMILED A RAINBOW OVERHEAD.

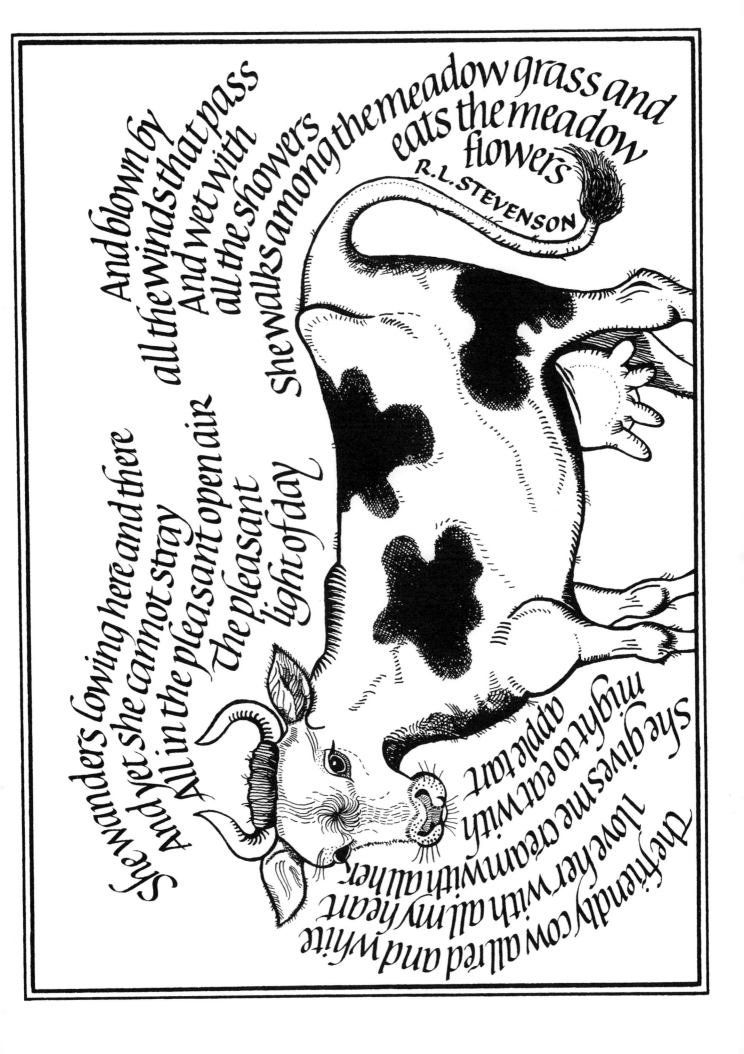

A is for
Armadillo

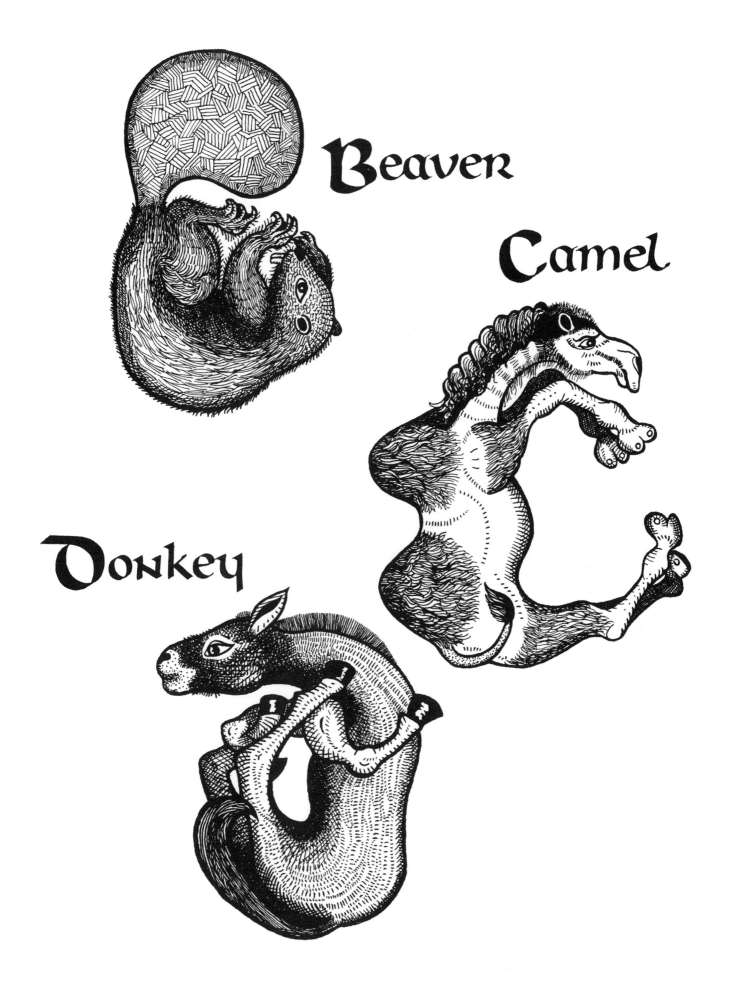

Beaver

Camel

Donkey

Elephant

Fox

Goat

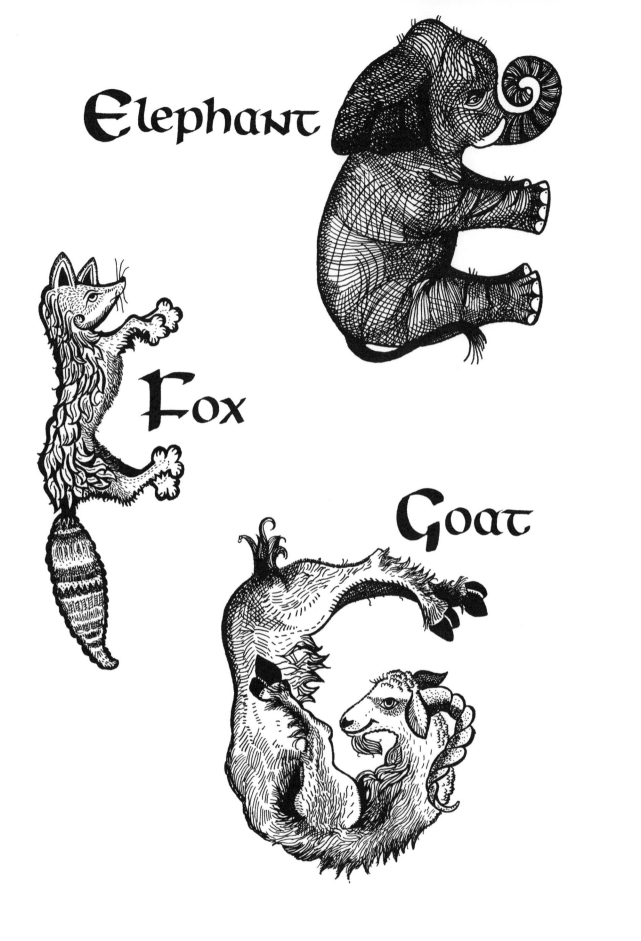

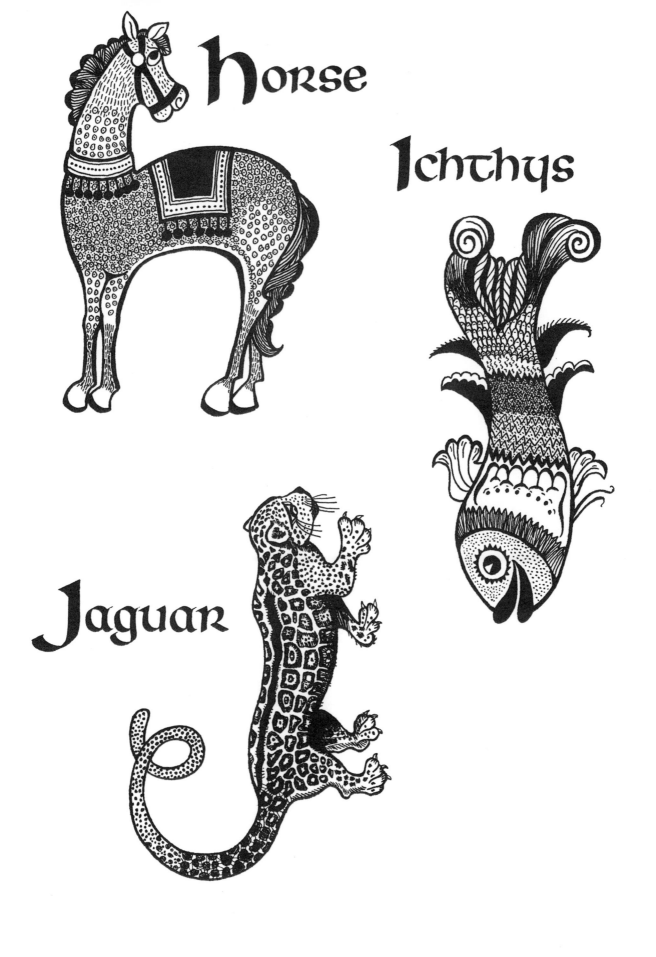

Horse

Ichthys

Jaguar

Kangaroo

Llama

Monkey

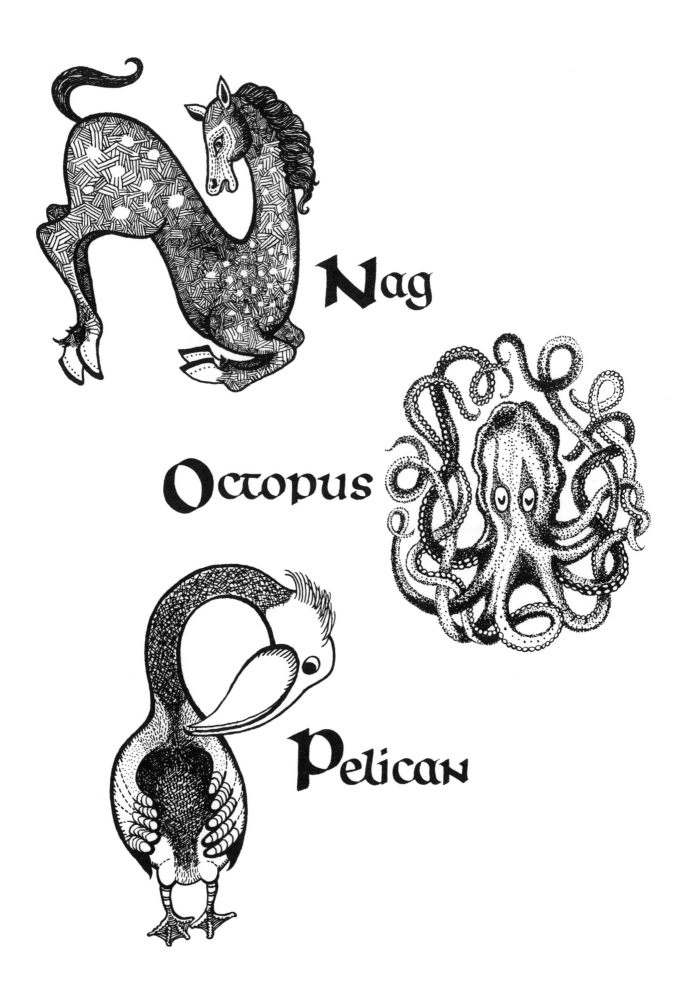

Nag

Octopus

Pelican

Quail

Raccoon

Sea horse

Tiger

Ursa

Viper

Warthog

X-ray fish

Yak

and Z is for
Zebra

The world is so
full of a number of things,
I'm sure we should all be
as happy as kings

R.L.STEVENSON

Designed by Barbara Holdridge
Composed by the Service Compostion Company,
  Baltimore, Maryland
Printed on 75-pound Williamsburg Offset and
  bound by United Graphics, Inc., Mattoon, Illinois